THE LURE OF THE RING

POWER, ADDICTION AND TRANSCENDENCE

IN

TOLKIEN'S THE LORD OF THE RINGS

BY

ALAN JAMES STRACHAN AND JANET COSTER

978-1-7323156-0-0

"Tolkien's Tom Bombadil echoes the deep joy and presence of any true mystic! His non-dual Being demonstrates the inherent strength that comes through identification with the earth and all living beings. *The Lure of the Ring* compellingly captures the essence of addiction, the seduction of power, and the nature of embodied spiritual transformation. I highly recommend this wise and engaging book."

—Richard Rohr, O.F.M.,
Founder of Center for Action and Contemplation

"The Lure of the Ring is one of those few books that honors and ignites the power and mystery of the interior life. It is an inspirational book that demonstrates how personal mythology directs our actions and organizes our experiences. Strachan and Coster provide an exceedingly accessible and comprehensive psychological-spiritual analysis of Tolkien's work, and how the human psyche can balance power, love, and integrity. A 'must read' as it is so relevant for human beings, individually and collectively at this time in history!"

—Angeles Arrien, Ph.D., Cultural Anthropologist, Author
of *The Second Half of Life and Living in Gratitude*

"The Lure of the Ring is a fascinating work, an exploration of the deeper meaning of Tolkien's Lord of the Rings. Drawing upon extensive immersion in both psychotherapy and Eastern philosophy, the authors find deep psychological insight in significant figures in the trilogy, especially in the evil narcissism of Sauron and the enlightened, non-dual awareness of Tom Bombadil. This short book takes us into the heart of Tolkien's genius showing levels of psychological and spiritual insight of which the great writer himself was unaware as he wrote Lord of the Rings but that he came to see in later life. Tolkien admirers have good reason to thank Alan Strachan and Janet Coster for their elegantly written and convincing reading of this 20th Century epic, and for their lucid analysis of its enduring relevance to all those on the path of personal growth and spiritual development."

> —Ralph White is the author of the memoir, *The Jeweled Highway: On the Quest for a Life of Meaning.* He is co-founder of the New York Open Center, the city's leading venue for holistic learning and world culture since 1984. He also directs the Esoteric Quest international conference series on the re-emergence of the Western Mystery Tradition. www.ralphwhite.net

"I was delighted to read your *Lure of the Ring* and feel your wisdom and love in how you presented Tolkien's beautiful literary character "Old Tom Bombadil." With a rich array of insights from transpersonal psychology and nondual spirituality, you have forged an easy portal for readers to enter the psyche and contemplate crucial topics, ranging from authentic/inauthentic use of power and healing core wounds, to mature wholeness and natural holiness in our True Identity."

> —Timothy Conway, author of *Women of Power & Grace* and the forthcoming works *The Liberating Zen Sourcebook, India's Sages,* and the extensive web-resource www.Enlightened-Spirituality.org

Old Tom

In shadow and moonlight,
Tom cradles the night . . .
In sunshine enchants
the wild forest with dance.
Though nameless, alone,
the wide world is his home;
at all times he expresses
a life lived as essence.
In silence he sings,
with freedom he flings
greening life with a flourish –
and we all are nourished.

Janet Coster

Acknowledgements

We are deeply grateful to Cynthia Blair for her inspired artwork in creating our cover illustration. We have been blessed by the encouragement and feedback from our dear friends, Francine Lapides, Howard Frankl, John Mizelle and Flo Mizelle.

Contents

Introduction

Tom Bombadil is the prevailing mystery in Tolkien's work. While almost every other aspect of Middle-earth is described for us in exacting detail, Tom is an enigma. We have almost no clue of his origins or his fate, his purpose or even what kind of being he is. It is no surprise that none of Tolkien's characters have attracted more discussion.

(Mark Fisher, The Riddle of Tom Bombadil)

Tom Bombadil was my favorite character when I read J.R.R. Tolkien's *The Lord of the Rings* in my early 20s. There was something deeply compelling about old Tom's spontaneity and independence of spirit, his visceral connectedness with the world, and his innate authority, that greatly appealed to me. Of all the characters in *The Lord of the Rings*, he was the only one who was deeply joyful, content, and wise, embracing yet also remaining a detached witness to the affairs of Men, Elves, Dwarves and the swirling drama of Middle-Earth. I suppose that I – not so joyful, not so content, and far from wise! – in some way longed to be like him.

Around that same time I also became completely enamored with the books anthropologist Carlos Castaneda wrote about the Yaqui Indian sorcerer don Juan. I spent three years devouring everything I could about shamanism, exploring the connections between don Juan's worldview and cross-cultural patterns of shamanic belief and behavior. I realize now that these two figures, Tom Bombadil and don Juan – a more unlikely pair would be hard to find – each represented for me an innate, embodied wisdom and a spiritual freedom grounded in the natural world.

Recently I returned to *The Lord of the Rings* and Tom Bombadil after a 30-year hiatus, inviting my wife Janet along for the ride. Each of us, by now, had experienced this riveting adventure more than once; this time we were prompted to re-enter Tolkien's doorway into Middle Earth because we were writing an essay about the nature of power, exploring the thesis that power is the truest test of character. We soon realized there was no better place to turn for an examination of power than Tolkien's *The Lord of the Rings.*

Tom Bombadil is an enigmatic character who was not included in Peter Jackson's movie trilogy of *The Lord of the Rings* despite the fact that many Tolkien scholars and en-thusiasts have found Bombadil to be unique, charismatic and intriguing. In Tolkien's epic he has singular powers and does not appear to belong to any of the races that popu-late Middle Earth. Many speculative essays have been writ-ten about Bombadil's nature and origins, with nothing approaching a consensus, and Tolkien himself deliberately remained vague.

Although we, too, are fascinated by "who Tom is," in *The Lure of the Ring* we make no attempt to determine where he "belongs" in Tolkien's imaginal universe. Instead, we highlight his singular – and, from a developmental and spir-itual perspective – transcendent being. This affords us the opportunity to explore, by contrast, the way in which other characters from *The Lord of the Rings* cope with the seductive influence of power as represented by the One Ring.

In Middle Earth, the Ring symbolizes and offers an overwhelming power to dominate, exerting a tantalizing and intoxicating pull on those in its proximity. Power deeply and innately seduces because it feeds the primary need of our ego-personalities to be in control, thereby attempting to assuage our manifold fears and insecurities. In Middle Earth, resisting the Ring's promise of power and domination becomes the ultimate test of the ego's addiction to control and, therefore, the ultimate test of character.

Throughout Tolkien's trilogy we see the power of the Ring to corrupt those who wish to possess it. *The Lure of the Ring* examines, from a psychodynamic perspective, the responses to the Ring of several of Tolkien's characters. It then locates them along a continuum of psychospiritual development, focusing principally on Sauron and Tom Bombadil and the contrast between them. The Dark Lord, Sauron, who utterly has succumbed to his craving for power, and who is completely identified with the Ring, resides at one end of this continuum. Occupying a middle ground are characters such as Galadriel, Gandalf the Wizard, and Frodo, each of whom heroically struggles against and, to varying degrees, resists the potent allure of the Ring. Then there is Tom Bombadil – at the other end of the continuum of psychospiritual development from Sauron – who operates from a radically different paradigm in relation to power and the Ring. (A case could be made that Bombadil's paradigm, i.e., his radically transformed identity, is so fundamentally different that he does not belong on the same continuum as Sauron. As we shall see, this kind of ambiguity – does he, or does he not, belong? – is characteristic of Bombadil, a being whose very nature is paradoxical and impossible to pin down with labels.)

Sauron is an example *par excellence* of a Hungry Ghost. Hungry Ghosts are denizens of one of the Six Realms of Existence in the Buddhist Wheel of Life. They are depicted as insubstantial, emaciated creatures with small mouths, scrawny necks, withered limbs and enormously bloated, empty bellies. Driven by a terrible, aching emptiness, mired in rage and anxiety, they live in perpetual misery because their desperate, addictive, wounded search for fulfillment brings no satisfaction. Propelled by such craving, pain and rage, Sauron-as-Hungry-Ghost mistakenly believes the Ring's power will save him, when in actuality his possessive, addictive search only perpetuates and amplifies his agony. The Ring is his "fix," but it never will satisfy his endless egoic lust for power. Seemingly potent and free, he is, in fact, painfully in bondage to his own deep, unacknowledged wounds and his sense of having lost power. By succumbing to his narcissistic yearning for dominance, and avoiding facing the traumatic pain – or core wound – that lies at the root of his reactivity, he only deepens his estrangement from his true Self.

The true Self – that we also refer to in *The Lure of the Ring* as the *unconditioned* or *undivided* Self – is present in each of us, and is alive beyond all stories, cravings and conditioning of our ego personality. It is a Self at one with the world, characterized by an inherent connectedness, peace and strength that have no fear-or-deficiency-based need to subjugate or wreak vengeance.

In contrast, the core wound is our point of greatest psychological vulnerability. It is the most excruciating narcissistic (i.e., egoic) injury that we experience, the place in which we feel wounded and powerless at the very core of our personal identity. The core wound experience is one of profound powerlessness, pain, deficiency and separateness. It is pain so acute and penetrating that it feels like our very identity is being annihilated, as though our life is on the line. It is the agonizing place where our ego selves innately feel the most alone and traumatized; it also is, therefore, the experience we try hardest to avoid, deny and protect. Nevertheless, despite our varied and rigorous personality defenses, it is not uncommon for the core wound to trigger intense narcissistic anger as the ego identity protects itself against its felt deficiencies by generating a desperate, rage-inflated sense of righteousness and potency. On the level of personality, the core wound is like a black hole exerting gravitational pull on everything around it.

The *core wound* and the *undivided self* can be viewed as two poles of identity, residing on opposite ends of a continuum of consciousness. The core wound fearfully *defends* individual identity, protecting itself by whatever means necessary. In contrast, the undivided self is liberated beyond individual identity – with nothing, therefore, to protect.

Sauron's obsessive, destructive, self-avoidant behavior is a vivid example of how mindlessly reacting to the inner agony of the core wound can shape a person's life. Out of a core sense of deficiency, Sauron seeks to compensate by acquiring power in order to dominate others. He has much to teach us about the pitfalls of becoming numb to our own core wound and then fruitlessly seeking to assuage, inflate, and defend ourselves by succumbing to blind, addictive cravings.

Unlike Sauron – or any other character in *The Lord of the Rings* – Tom Bombadil fully embodies the *undivided* or *unconditioned* Self. His identity is paradoxical: although he has a character structure, he is not identified with the attachments and addictive passions of his ego personality. Rather, when asked who he is, he replies that he is who we all are when we are alone, and silent. He is silence; he is nameless; he is formless presence or consciousness; he is Being itself.

Tom Bombadil's true nature proves to be a fascinating and illuminating exploration. Tom's inherent connectedness and goodwill, his joy, his complete immersion in the present, his lack of fear, his utter disinterest in power, and his humble respect for life eloquently reflects to each of us the joyful resting in and as Being itself that is the essential truth of Who we all are.

Alan Strachan with Janet Coster

CHAPTER 1

Galadriel is Tested by The One Ring

One of the most compelling scenes in Peter Jackson's visually arresting film version of Tolkien's *The Lord of the Rings* occurs when Frodo the Hobbit and his Fellowship-of-the-Ring companions pause during their perilous journey to spend a night amongst the elves. Frodo has been entrusted with guarding and destroying the One Ring created by the Dark Lord Sauron for the purpose of seizing dominion over Middle-Earth. Sauron's power is growing and Frodo's harrowing quest to destroy the One Ring – and thereby prevent Sauron from acquiring such dominion – is in grave danger.

Galadriel, the Lady of the Wood and Queen of the Elves, glides by in the dark of night, and Frodo awakens. Following her, she leads him to a mirror that can be used to foretell the future. Gazing into the mirror, Frodo sees a horrifying vision: the enslavement of the Hobbits by Sauron and the destruction of their beautiful Shire. Galadriel tells him that this vision "is what will come to pass, if you should fail. The

Fellowship is breaking, it has already begun. He will try to take the Ring, you know of whom I speak. One by one, it will destroy them."

Frodo can feel how resisting the corrupting power of the Ring already has begun to wear on him. He tells Galadriel, "If you ask it of me, I will give you the One Ring." He holds out his hand, palm up, and on it rests the golden Ring of Power. Only twice before – when Frodo's Uncle Bilbo offered it to him, and when Frodo himself offered it to Gandalf the Wizard – has someone offered to permanently relinquish the powerful and seductive Ring.

"You offer it to me freely?" Galadriel says with surprise, and slowly approaches Frodo. Her hand is shaking as she reaches towards the Ring. Her voice suddenly resonant, throaty with feeling, she says, "I do not deny that my heart has greatly desired this." A darkness begins to envelop them. Frodo looks at her, eyes wide, brow slightly furrowed.

Galadriel raises her arms high above her head. Her voice rises to a shriek as she declares, "IN THE PLACE OF A DARK LORD, YOU WOULD HAVE A QUEEN!" A wind whips her hair and garments and the darkness thickens. Her voice becomes deep and powerful, and her eyes shine with an unearthly glow, "NOT DARK BUT BEAUTIFUL AND TERRIBLE AS THE MORN!"

Fearful, Frodo takes a few involuntary steps backward.

"TREACHEROUS AS THE SEAS! STRONGER THAN THE FOUNDATIONS OF THE EARTH! ALL SHALL LOVE ME AND DESPAIR!"

Abruptly she stops. The preternatural light returns to normal, as do Galadriel's features, "I have passed the test," she says quietly, handing back the ring. "I will diminish, and go into the West, and remain Galadriel."

In this precipitous moment, Galadriel has learned something of surpassing importance: that she has inner strength to turn down the opportunity to wield ultimate power.

Frodo plaintively tells her, "I cannot do this alone."

"You are a Ring-bearer, Frodo. To bear a Ring of Power is to be alone." She extends her hand to him. "This task was appointed to you, and if you do not find a way, no one will."

"I know what I must do, it's just that . . . I'm afraid to do it."

Galadriel bends down to speak to him at eye level, "Even the smallest person can change the course of the future."

Galadriel, having refused ultimate power for herself, goes one step further: wisely she empowers Frodo with the knowledge that, though he might feel small and afraid by comparison with Sauron and the Ring of Power, he nevertheless has the strength within him to succeed. When they part she bestows upon him a small vial, a further precious gift. "I give you the light of Eärendil, our most beloved star. May it be a light for you in dark places, when all other lights go out." (Walsh, Jackson and Boyens, 2001, pages 103-104)

It is not simply Galadriel's position of authority amongst the elves that allows her to give this second gift. More significantly, she is passing on to Frodo a symbol of the strength of character she has demonstrated in her own struggle with the One Ring, i.e., the strength to find light in the midst of terrible darkness.

CHAPTER 2

The Ring as a Measure
Of Character

There is wisdom in Lord Acton's well-known assertion that "power corrupts, and absolute power corrupts absolutely." Power is seductive because it feeds the core need of our ego personality to be in control. Control assuages the fear and insecurity of the ego, nurturing its narcissism. The greater the power, the greater the opportunity – and therefore the temptation – to do whatever we want. Thus "absolute" power particularly is seductive because it feeds our narcissistic desire to have godlike control.

Abraham Lincoln observed, "If you want to test a man's character, give him power." In The Lord of the Rings, ultimate power, and therefore the ultimate test of character, is represented by the One Ring created by Sauron. The Ring of Power exerts a nearly irresistible pull, and throughout the story many are tested by its corrupting influence.

Galadriel's battle to resist the allure of the Ring is a vivid depiction of the way in which power can begin to seduce and corrupt. In her case, however, she has the strength to resist the temptation. Previously, Gandalf, too, showed great wisdom and restraint when he refused Frodo's offer of the Ring:

> "No! With that power I should have power too great and terrible. And over me the Ring would gain a power still greater and more deadly! Do not tempt me! For I do not wish to become like the Dark Lord himself. Yet the way of the Ring to my heart is by pity, pity for weakness and the desire of strength to do good. Do not tempt me! I dare not take it, not even to keep it safe, unused. The wish to wield it would be too great for my strength."
>
> (Tolkien, 1965a, pages 70-1)

In earlier chapters of the Ring's history, we also discover that a young boy named Sméagol was not so wise, and that he succumbed to the dark power of the Ring, killing his friend Déagol to gain possession of it. Under its baleful influence, Sméagol eventually degenerated into Gollum, a miserable, pitiable creature utterly obsessed with desire to reclaim his "Precious," the Ring. So, too, the Ringwraiths were altered by the Ring into the undead Nazgûl. They were at one time the nine Kings of men but, blinded by greed and power, they became Sauron's "most terrible servants; darkness went with them, and they cried with the voices of death." (Tolkien, 2002, page 346) Again and again we see the power of the Ring corrupting those who seek to possess it, turning them to evil even if their original intention is to use it toward noble ends.

The psychospiritual development of the characters in The Lord of the Rings can be assessed by their response to the Ring. At one end is the Dark Lord, Sauron, who utterly has succumbed to his craving for power, and who is completely identified with the Ring. Then there are characters such as Galadriel, Gandalf the Wizard, and Frodo, each of whom mightily struggles against and, to varying degrees, resists the allure of the Ring. Later on, we will see – at an entirely different level of psychospiritual development – Tom Bombadil. He, and he alone, functions from a unique and radical paradigm in relation to power and the Ring.

CHAPTER 3

Sauron's Blinding Rage

Sauron is a perfect example of someone who becomes lost in the convoluted corridors of the ego personality. Trapped in impotence, compelled by painful narcissistic wounds, blinded by desire, he gives vent to his frustration and rage through an overwhelming need for tyranny and revenge. Sauron's overwhelming army can be seen as a symbol of the offensive and defensive structure that surrounds all of our core wounds. Whatever our personality style, we all have ways by which we defend, project onto, and attack others. Whenever any of us feels wounded and powerless at the core of our identity, like Sauron, it is natural to want to turn the tables on those whom we believe have oppressed or betrayed us. Opportunity for vengeance provides one of the greatest temptations to use power.

Over time, Sauron utterly has lost touch with his true Self. Now he only sees the world through the narrow aperture – aptly depicted as the "Eye of Sauron" – of his raging, wounded narcissism. Ironically, Sauron's "all-seeing" Eye is blind to any understanding of the twisted and destructive nature of his thirst for power and vengeance. When Frodo gazes into the Eye in Galadriel's mirror, here is what he sees:

> . . . suddenly the Mirror went altogether dark, as dark as if a hole had opened in the world of sight, and Frodo looked into emptiness. In the black abyss there appeared a single Eye that slowly grew, until it filled nearly all the Mirror. So terrible was it that Frodo stood rooted, unable to cry out or to withdraw his gaze. The Eye was rimmed with fire, but was itself glazed, yellow as a cat's, watchful and intent, and the black slit of its pupil opened on a pit, a window into nothing.
>
> (Tolkien, 1965a, page 379)

"A window into nothing" is an apt description of the emptiness of Sauron's narcissistic and false self.

Significantly, Sauron did not begin his existence as a "Dark Lord." Instead, as Tolkien observes about Sauron in one of his letters, "Very slowly, beginning with fair motives . . . he becomes a reincarnation of Evil, and a thing lusting for Complete Power – and so consumed ever more fiercely with hate . . ." (Carpenter, 1981, page 151) It is important, therefore, to understand that Sauron begins, with "fair motives," by wanting to improve and reform Middle Earth. However, although initially he feels the desire to serve others in this way, gradually he cannot help but succumb to his all-consuming egoic need for dominance, ultimately seeking, through violence, to become the ruler of the world. Thwarted in prior attempts to have gained far-reaching power, Sauron's rage grows stronger. A vicious cycle takes shape. The pain of previous defeat and rejection further inflames his all-consuming narcissistic wound. This downward spiral of rejection, pain, and anger increases his desire to exact retribution; vengeance and domination become imagined means of redemption. The more Sauron commits himself to this obsessive path, the more alienated he becomes from his true Self and any true sense of connection.

Who of us cannot relate to this on some level? Ambition and desire, met with rejection, can trigger deep, seemingly unbearable pain, followed by fantasies of regaining control in order to feel valuable and honored. Who has not imagined seeking some measure of vengeance on those who have wounded us, in order to salve our wounds and regain a sense of control? Ultimately, Sauron sacrifices his life to this voracious cycle of feelings, eventually leading to his demise.

Tolkien provides a crucial clue to these psychodynamics of Sauron's downfall, telling us that ". . . it had been his virtue (and therefore also the cause of his fall, and of his relapse) that he loved order and co-ordination, and disliked all confusion and wasteful friction." Tolkien adds that although Sauron's ". . . original desire for 'order' had really envisaged the good estate (especially physical well-being) of his 'subjects'" [eventually] ". . . his 'plans', the idea coming from his own isolated mind, became the sole object of his will, and an end, the End, in itself." (Tolkien, 1993, pages 396, 397)

Tolkien's reflections help to elucidate Sauron's two principle personality traits: First, there is his *perfectionism,* which leads to an intolerance of anything that does not conform to his idealized image of how things should be. His fundamentalist desire to impose his version of order on the world and its inhabitants grows into an all-consuming obsession, until he no longer cares what means he employs to achieve his ends. Sauron is desperate to create what he thinks would be a perfect world, a world made in his own image.

Second, Sauron's perfectionism goes hand-in-hand with his out-of-control *narcissism.* Tolkien's description of Sauron's "idea coming from his own isolated mind" becoming "an end . . . in itself" is the very image of Narcissus, the mythological Greek youth who was cursed to fall in love with his own reflection and ultimately was doomed by his obsession.

There is a vast and crucial difference between believing that one can *create a perfect world* (which is, of course, impossible), and *paying "perfect" attention to the world as it is,* with all its "flaws." The belief that one can create a perfect world, i.e., a world that conforms to our personal notions of order, is an immature narcissistic fantasy.

However, paying "perfect" attention – i.e., clearly and unsparingly attending to whatever arises in our moment-to-moment experience, without projecting our concepts, needs and feelings onto it – is another matter entirely. "Perfectly" perceiving the world as it is, whether or not we like what we see, is a mark of psychospiritual maturity.

CHAPTER 4

Narcissistic Rage

Thwarted and infuriated by the failure of his perfectionist desire to conform Middle Earth to his will, Sauron's life becomes an unending expression of narcissistic rage. Narcissistic rage, which is different from other forms of anger, can be triggered when an individual has suffered the deepest developmental wounding to their ego personality – a core wound / narcissistic injury so intense and acute that it feels as though one's very existence is threatened. Narcissistic injury of this type first occurs for us all in childhood, and it can be re-triggered many times throughout our lives, leaving us open to a profound sense of vulnerability, deficiency and isolation, which we then hide, protect and defend at all costs. Our personality structure and style, in part, serves as our particular "flavor" of defense. Almaas writes that such a wound,

> . . . has special characteristics because the narcissistic hurt is different from other types of emotional pain. The fact that this hurt is very vulnerable, and opens up to an emptiness signifying the dissolution of

identity, imbues the reactive anger with an intensity and hardness rarely seen in other kinds of anger.

(Almaas, 1996, page 324)

Furthermore,

The rage may turn into, or be accompanied by, a cold hatred that gives . . . qualities of power, invincibility, and calculation. This hatred underlies the desire for vengeance, for wanting to inflict pain and suffering, and for actually enjoying getting back at the person who failed [you].

(Almaas, 1996, page 327)

"Cold hatred . . . power, invincibility, and calculation" all are qualities readily attributable to Sauron. Such narcissistic rage may be triggered by many circumstances, including an experience of "conspicuous defeat," (Kohut, 1978, page 638) a condition of particular significance for Sauron since twice he had been defeated in his attempts at world conquest prior to events related in *The Lord of the Rings.*

CHAPTER 5

The Significance of
The One Ring

Sauron originally forged the One Ring in the volcanic fires of Mount Doom in order to control other Rings of Power that were held by the Elves, Dwarves and Men. Sauron's desire, according to Tolkien, was to use the One Ring "to establish a control over the mind and wills of his servants." (Carpenter, 1981, page 153) His quest to further his domination, Tolkien tells us, meant that Sauron ". . . had been obliged to let a great part of his own inherent power . . . pass into the One Ring." (Carpenter, 1981, page 153) Thus, Sauron becomes inextricably identified with – and as – the One Ring. From a psychological perspective, he has created the Ring by projecting into it the "power" of his narcissistic rage.

The Ring of Power, then, is a symbol, a mirror, an embodiment, and an amplification of Sauron's core wound rage, hatred and desire for revenge.

Whoever bears the Ring, therefore, will feel the infused weight of Sauron's wound, and, resonating with it, their own core wound. The Ring draws upon and amplifies each Ring-bearer's innate narcissistic wish to have power to satisfy every egoic desire, including power to crush and destroy anyone who ever has betrayed, or caused pain, to the bearer. This seductive urge strongly compels the Ring-bearer to take the path of domination, albeit at the expense of his or her soul. It is no wonder the Ring hangs so heavily on the spirit of any and all who carry it, including Frodo.

It is natural to feel the need to dominate others when one inwardly feels victimized and deficient from one's early core wounding. Sauron exemplifies the all-too-familiar process of being caught in this personal victim story, which then leads to responding in an unconscious, knee-jerk manner to the agonizing feelings, images and thoughts of one's inadequacy and ill-treatment. The alternative path, so challenging to follow, would be to choose to "look into" the Ring-as-mirror, an option that offers the opportunity of embracing, transforming and healing the agony of one's own narcissistic injury with its intrinsic sense of deficiency. To do so makes it possible to have a direct sense of our unconditioned and undivided self that lies beneath, prior to and beyond this drama of personal identity.

CHAPTER 6

The Dark Lord as Hungry Ghost

Paradoxically, the Ring symbolizes Sauron's greatest sense of power – derived from rage-induced grandiosity – and his greatest weakness, i.e., an utter unwillingness to confront the narcissistic injury underlying his rage. Bereft of the Ring, he feels he is not whole, *yet ironically he chases after this very symbol of his deepest experience of separation and pain.*

Sauron is a perfect exemplar, for us all, of the addictive process, classically represented by the Hungry Ghosts who inhabit one of the Six Realms of Existence described in the Buddhist Wheel of Life.

The Hungry Ghosts are probably the most vividly drawn metaphors in the Wheel of Life. Phantomlike creatures with withered limbs, grossly bloated bellies, and long thin necks, the Hungry Ghosts in many ways represent a fusion of rage and desire. Tormented by unfulfilled cravings and insatiably demanding of impossible satisfactions, the Hungry Ghosts are searching for gratification for old unful- filled needs whose time has passed. They are beings who have uncovered a terrible emptiness within themselves, who cannot see the impossibility of cor- recting something that has already happened. Their ghostlike state represents their attachment to the past.

In addition, these beings, all impossibly hungry and thirsty, cannot drink or eat without causing themselves terrible pain or indigestion. The very at- tempts to satisfy themselves cause more pain. Their long, thin throats are so narrow and raw that swal- lowing produces unbearable burning and irritation. Their bloated bellies are in turn unable to digest nourishment; attempts at gratification only yield a more intense hunger and craving. These are beings who cannot take in a present-day, albeit transitory, satisfaction. They remain obsessed with the fantasy of achieving complete relief from the pain of their past and are stubbornly unaware that their desire is fantasy. It is this knowledge that such people are es- tranged from, for their fantasy must be owned as fantasy. The Hungry Ghosts must come in contact with the ghostlike nature of their own longings.

(Epstein, 1995, pages 28-29)

Sauron, like any addict, desperately needs his fix, believing it will assuage his pain, when in reality it offers only tem- porary distraction and numbing. His addictive search for the Ring of Power is painful, for it enhances and aggra- vates the inner burning ache of his core wound. His quest serves only to accentuate his wraith-like emptiness and agonizing craving. Recovering the Ring never will end Sauron's pain or bring him peace, and yet obsessively he seeks it, believing it will save him. The blindness of his Self-negating quest only takes him closer to his doom – symbolized, fittingly, by Mt. Doom.

CHAPTER 7

Destroying The Ring

Sauron's power instantly is broken as soon as the Ring is in the fires of Mt. Doom. Tolkien evocatively captures Sauron's demise:

> The earth groaned and quaked. The Towers of the Teeth swayed, tottered, and fell down; the mighty ramparts crumbled; the Black Gate was hurled in ruin; and from far away, now dim, now growing, now mounting to the clouds, there came a drumming rumble, a roar, a long echoing roll of ruinous noise.
>
> (Tolkien, 1965b, page 227)

Then:

> "The Power that drove them [i.e., Sauron's army] on and filled them with hate and fury was wavering, its will was removed from them . . ."
>
> (Tolkien, 1965b, page 226)

Mount Doom's fiery volcano is a potent symbol both for the creation and the destruction of the One Ring. Narcissistic rage is an all-consuming fire in the heart, a fire that forges ". . . heightened sadism . . . the need for revenge" and ". . . the deeply anchored, unrelenting compulsion in the pursuit of all these aims . . ." (Kohut, 1978, pages 639, 638) In the end, however, the voracious fire of narcissistic rage ultimately consumes itself. This is Sauron's fate, a psychological form of self-immolation. It is a fate that, according to Tolkien, "he never contemplated nor feared," blinded as he is by an inflated belief in his invulnerability. (Carpenter, 1981, page 153) It is the fate of any of us who only lash out from, and never transform, our pain.

The paradoxical quality of blind rage – i.e., that it can imbue a feeling of immense power even as it carries the seeds of its own destruction – is captured evocatively by Frederick Buechner:

> Of the Seven Deadly Sins, anger is possibly the most fun. To lick your wounds, to smack your lips over grievances long past, to roll over your tongue the prospect of bitter confrontations still to come, to savor to the last toothsome morsel both the pain you are given and the pain you are giving back – in many ways it is a feast fit for a king. The chief drawback is that what you are wolfing down is yourself. The skeleton at the feast is you.
>
> (Buechner, 1973, page 2)

Sauron's true inner weakness is openly revealed once the Ring is destroyed. The One Ring represents the artifice of Sauron's ego personality: golden and shiny on its exterior, it is nevertheless constructed upon Sauron's unexamined and desperate desire for control and vengeance. The shaky scaffolding upon which Sauron's ego personality is built collapses when the Ring is consumed in the fires of Mt. Doom. He is, sadly, only a Hungry Ghost, and the destruction of his Ring reveals Sauron's "power" to have been a house of cards. His is a reactive power that is not derived from true strength. True strength is garnered through humble willingness to receive and feel whatever life brings, no matter how painful or infuriating, and no matter how tempting, instead, to exact our vengeance. Sauron has not displayed this strength of embracing life's pain and disappointments; rather, he has demonstrated an inability and persistent unwillingness to face his inner wounding. Having recoiled from acquiring a clear understanding about, and transformation of, the pain that lies at the root of his reactivity, he instead succumbs to narcissistic rage.

The Ring – as symbol of Sauron's narcissistic wound – is his life, his *raison d'etre* on the level of ego personality. Once his purpose is taken from him, little else can survive, because everything Sauron has sought has derived from the hollow corridors of his inner impoverishment.

Aside from Sauron's fate as described in the context of *The Lord of the Rings*, on a psychospiritual level there remains the possibility that Sauron – as any one of us – could learn from his disastrous ego-driven campaign to command the world. If he were willing to develop humility, and to look unsparingly at the root cause of his lust for endless power, he could find healing for his narcissistic wound and the rage it generates. By doing so he would develop true inner strength, rather than an artifice of power. He then could move through the world with a sense of inherent sufficiency, rather than desperately, addictively trying to consume the world in order to compensate for his agonizing inner emptiness.

CHAPTER 8

Sauron as Everyman
A Character Summary

Sauron is a graphic depiction of someone who resides at the lower end of the spectrum of psychospiritual development. He is a compulsive addict, and his addiction is one that is common, to varying degrees, to us all: he is addicted to his ego personality's passion for control. Despite the great destructive power that he wields, Sauron – in terms of true character – is very weak. We have seen how he is the epitome of a Hungry Ghost, the blind victim of uncontrolled appetite. Ostensibly powerful and free, in fact he is in painful bondage to his own unacknowledged wounds. Deeply split off from his essential connection to the world, feeling incomplete, empty, and out of control, he sees no avenue other than violence as the means to salve his wounds. He is the embodiment of an ego personality descending into madness and annihilation by utterly giving in to narcissistic craving for dominion.

In Tolkien's story, the Eye of Sauron is the lens through which he scans the world, a hypervigilant compulsion driven by desperation, and rage. But everything Sauron "sees" is filtered and distorted by his obsessive urges. No matter how far afield he casts his Eye, he cannot escape the shadow of his own inner torment, a suffering that colors all of his perceptions. In the final analysis, Sauron's Eye best could serve as a mirror reflecting him back to himself, but that is the one place he will not seek truth.

We have noted how Sauron began as one who apparently wants to serve and bring positive change to the world; however, overtaken by his perfectionist desire to dictate and control, in the end he demands that others serve him. Utterly obsessed with his own needs, violent and manipulative toward everyone else, his originally lofty goal degenerates into subjugation through destruction and propagation of fear. It is sobering to register how often we have witnessed this perversion of good intentions in the history of our own world beyond Middle Earth.

Tolkien observed that Sauron "Eventually . . . squandered his power (of being) in the endeavor to gain control of others." (Tolkien, 1993, page 394) "Power of being" is true power, for it does not require power over others, only mastery of oneself.

To understand more about this kind of "power," let us now turn to the most enigmatic character in *The Lord of the Rings:* Tom Bombadil. Of all the characters in *The Lord of the Rings, Tom Bombadil is the only one completely disinterested in power.* This makes him extremely unusual from a psychospiritual perspective. Tom Bombadil alone represents someone who lives and recognizes himself as the *unconditioned* Self, i.e., unlike most of us, he is not identified with, and as, his ego personality. Let us examine how his attributes support this interpretation.

CHAPTER 9

Tom's True Name is Silence

In the first volume of *The Lord of the Rings*, Tom Bombadil rescues two of Frodo's Hobbit companions from the lethal intent of Old Man Willow. Inviting all four Hobbits to be his guests, Tom bounds off, singing, in the direction of his home, while they scramble to follow. Once the Hobbits reach Tom's home, they meet his enchanting wife, Goldberry. Taking advantage of Tom's momentary absence, Frodo – who is intensely curious about Tom – addresses Goldberry,

> *"Fair lady! Tell me, if my asking does not seem foolish, who is Tom Bombadil?"*
>
> *"He is," said Goldberry, staying her swift movements and smiling.*
>
> (Tolkien, 1965a, page 135)

Strangely, for one who is so hospitable, Goldberry inexplicably appears not to have answered Frodo, but in fact she has said quite precisely who Tom is:

He – *IS*.

This unorthodox reply provides us with a crucial clue about Tom's identity. Goldberry is telling Frodo that Tom's true nature, his direct experience and understanding of who he is, has nothing to do with a name – is, in fact, *beyond* naming.

It is important to understand the psychological development of selfhood in order to understand how this could be so. Each of us develops an individual ego personality partly through internalizing and identifying with aspects of our environment. Gradually all of the things we collectively align with come to constitute a sense of "me." As this occurs, we feel we are able to complete the sentence "I am" in a number of ways. "I am an American citizen," "I am a teacher," "I am a taxpayer," "I am a baseball fan," and so forth. Our *summary* statement – the shorthand version of all of these assimilations – is to identify with our name. We say, "I am Jim Smith" or "I am Sarah Perkins" and, for us, this symbolizes the sum of our personal identifications.

We are very attached to this way of naming and understanding ourselves. Thus, at the level of personality or ego we strongly believe ourselves to be all that which we have introjected and named as ourselves. Our belief is so strong and habitual, in fact, that we don't even give it a second thought. However, if we move forward on a path of psychospiritual maturation, we begin to loosen our attachment with such namings. We begin to recognize – on a deeper level of truth – that we have a paradoxical identity that is both personal (that is to say, comprised of our usual associations), and transpersonal (completely free of any and all identifications, even while being intimately, inherently connected to all of life).

One of the pioneers of transpersonal psychology, Jack

Engler, famously said, "You have to be somebody before you can be nobody." (Engler, 1993, page 119) He was describing the path to psychospiritual maturation. Being "somebody," that is, believing that we are, in fact, the sum of all of our self-cataloguing, does represent a certain necessary level of development. At the same time, embracing the wisdom that we *are not* truly defined by these many identifications expresses a further level of personal growth and understanding. This is the transpersonal stage of psychospiritual development as represented by Tom Bombadil. Tom's core "identification" is that he does not identify with any name, quality, behavior, or any other affiliation. *Therein lies his deep and essential freedom.*

In a later scene, we discover Tom recounting for the Hobbits many fascinating and miraculous tales of the world, and Frodo tries, once again, to find out "who" he is.

> The Hobbits sat still before him, enchanted; it seemed as if, under the spell of his words, the wind had gone, and the clouds had dried up, and the day had been withdrawn, and darkness had come from East and West, and all the sky was filled with the light of white stars.
>
> Whether the morning and evening of one day or many days had passed Frodo could not tell. He did not feel either hungry or tired, only filled with wonder. The stars shone through the window and the silence of heavens seemed to be around him. He spoke at last out of his wonder and a sudden fear of that silence:
>
> "Who are you, master?" he asked.

"Eh, what?" said Tom sitting up, his eyes glinting in the gloom. "Don't you know my name yet? That's the only answer. Tell me, who are you, alone, yourself and nameless?

(Tolkien, 1965a, page 142)

What does Tom mean when he asks, "Don't you know my name yet?" and then says, "That's the only answer"? The *only* answer to which he refers can only be the *silence* in between his two sentences:

"Don't you know my name yet?"

[Pause. Silence.]

"That's the only answer."

Goldberry earlier had tried to tell Frodo that Tom's true name is silence. Tom, too, is telling them this, and the Hobbits have sat with him, immersed in the immensity of silence. Next, Tom reframes his answer in a more overt manner, turning the tables and asking Frodo, "Tell me, who are you, alone, yourself and nameless?"

Tom's true name is that he has no name. He is nameless. Moreover, his reply is more an invitation than a question. He is letting Frodo know that silence is *his* – Frodo's – own true name as well. He calls Frodo toward a deeper participation with reality, i.e., to know that we are all, in the essence of our being, without name. This is the truest seeing of anyone at the deepest level of spiritual truth: We *are*. We *exist*. Who we are is beyond naming, surpassing all expression – we are Being itself.

Eckhart Tolle has remarked, "Your innermost sense of self, of who you are ... is the *I Am* that is deeper than name and form." (Tolle, 2006, page 21) In any individual's life, prior to the creation of an identity, and prior to the creation of the world as seen through that identity, there is this *unconditioned* consciousness – pure awareness without judgment, interpretation, or separation.

Attached as we are to the solidity and reassurance of our many identifications, the notion that we are deeper than name and form can be challenging to comprehend and embrace. In psychospiritual terms, Tom Bombadil is a representation of consciousness itself, even while he also is "Tom." He represents – and mirrors – a paradox of human identity and existence. On the one hand, clearly he has a developed and idiosyncratic personality, a character structure. On the other hand, when asked who he is, he answers that he is who we all are when we are alone, and silent. Prior to any acquisition of words and the development of individual identity, Tom is – *we all are* – primordial, ontological, Silence. Moreover – as Tom tries to point out to Frodo – we are that silence still, even when we have come strictly to believe we are an individual self.

The Indian sage Nisargadatta provides an example of identity that knows itself simply as "I am." Nisargadatta meditated for several years on the phrase "I am" at the instruction of his spiritual teacher. He credits this practice with transcendence of his personal identity.

> My guru told me . . . go back to that state of pure being, where the "I am" is still in its purity, before it got contaminated with "this I am" or "that I am." Your burden is of false identifications – abandon them all. . . . I simply followed his instruction which was to focus the mind on pure being "I am," and

stay in it. I used to sit for hours together, with nothing but the "I am" in my mind and soon peace and joy and a deep all-embracing love became my normal state. In it all disappeared – myself, my Guru, the life I lived, the world around me. Only peace remained and unfathomable silence.

(Nisargadatta, 2005, page 239)

On another occasion, when asked by a student, "How to find the way to one's own being?," Nisargadatta responds. "Give up all questions except one: 'Who am I'? After all, the only fact you are sure of is that you are. The 'I am' is certain. The 'I am this' is not. Struggle to find out what you are in reality." (Nisargadatta, 2005, page 70)

When Nisargadatta immerses himself in "I am," and when Tom reflects on who he is, "alone . . . and nameless," each understands their true name to be "unfathomable silence."

Tom further addresses Frodo's "Who are you?" question, by saying:

But you are young and I am old. Eldest, that's what I am. Mark my words, my friends: Tom was here before the river and the trees; Tom remembers the first raindrop and the first acorn. He made the paths before the Big People, and saw the little People arriving. He was here before the Kings and the graves and the Barrow-wights. When the Elves passed westward, Tom was here already, before the seas were bent. He knew the dark under the stars when it was fearless – before the Dark Lord came from outside."

(Tolkien, 1965a, page 142)

Tom compassionately says, "But you are young and old," in recognition that Frodo is too young and unformed at this stage of his life to have the wisdom ultimately will allow him to understand that, like Tom, his true name is silence. Frodo's discomfort with this level of truth is evident when, moments earlier, he has spoken to Tom "out of his wonder and *a sudden fear of that silence.*"

Tom has answered Frodo's "Who are you?" question in two ways: *In terms of identity,* Tom's true name is silence. Simultaneously, *in relationship to Frodo* – and, indeed, to all others – we shall see that he is called Eldest.

CHAPTER 10

Tom Can't be Caught

There is an occasion when Goldberry offers another enigmatic reply when she describes Tom to Frodo and his companions, saying: "No one has ever caught old Tom walking in the forest, wading in the water, leaping on the hilltops under light and shadow." (Tolkien, 1965a, page 135)

What can she mean by this?

When Goldberry says that "no one has ever caught Old Tom," she is describing something far more significant than someone physically catching him. She is referring, once again, to the nature of his true "identity" and his level of psychospiritual development. One who knows himself to be nameless and beyond form cannot be "caught" in the same manner by which the rest of us – mired in attachments – are so easily snared. Consider for a moment this wonderful Zen saying:

The wild geese do not intend to cast their reflection,
The water has no mind to receive their image.

The wild geese cast a reflection, but they neither intend to, nor are they concerned about, the reflection they cast. Wild geese just – *are*. They simply are *being* wild geese. The water reflects the image of the geese, but it is not waiting for the opportunity to do so nor does it hold on to the reflection as it passes. The water just – *is*. It simply is *being* water.

This Zen saying reminds us that, in the realm of true being, we simply *are*. However, in the realm of our ego-mind – where we live self-consciously aware of, and deeply invested in, our numerous daily identifications, and where *doing* is more important than *being* – we are quite concerned about the image we cast. In the realm of ego-mind, if someone reflects back to us an image of ourselves that we do not like because it does not match our preferred image, we get "caught" – caught by our strong attachment to being seen in a particular way.

"Tom Bombadil" cannot be caught in the way the ego-mind and personality can be caught because he is not ego-ically concerned about the image he casts. He simply is. Responding completely to the fullness and freedom of each moment, he is one with life without clinging to it. Tom cannot be caught because, dwelling in and as the essential Self, "he" is not "there" to be caught.

CHAPTER 11

Tom is Timeless

Understanding Tom Bombadil is an exercise in paradox. So far, we have seen that he has a name yet is nameless, that he simply *is* – yet is not there to be caught. It should come as no surprise, then, to discover that Tom also has a paradoxical relationship with time.

Tom lives both inside and outside of time. When referring to his life inside of time, he calls himself "Eldest," thereby indicating his relative age in comparison with other living beings. Inside the chronological unfolding of time, Tom has been alive the longest.

Paradoxically Tom also says of himself, "He knew the dark under the stars when it was fearless – before the Dark Lord came from outside." (Tolkien, 1965a, page 42) "The dark under the stars when it was fearless" refers to undivided consciousness, a stage in which the world is One, before the ego personality splits the world into self and other. Once there is awareness of our self as individual and separate, then time is measured sequentially, for now there is a self to measure the sequence of events. Once we become a separate self, then we become aware that our separate self will end, which gives rise to time as well as to fear. In contrast, the undivided self both is timeless and fearless, for there is nothing to measure and no self to protect.

In the *undivided* state, time always is *now* – we simply *are*. We are undivided, and time is undivided. For the *separate* self, time becomes compartmentalized, as we ourselves are compartmentalized: the *past* is what we remember happened to us, the *future* is what we hope for and fear, and awareness of the *present* tends to be chronically compromised by shifting tides of self-centered thoughts and feelings, perpetually reacting to a remembered past and an imagined future.

This is the paradox of time: Mortal, we long for eternity, gazing longingly at the infinite span of years, assuming that is where eternity lies – when actually it is, already, here. NOW. Instead of looking ahead, or being caught by the past, if we fully enter each present moment, undivided, then all sense of time's passage drops away and we abide in the eternal, infinite Now. This is the *enantiodromia* of time: that *the moment itself is eternal.*

Tom's identity is paradoxical; so too is his relationship with time:

On the one hand, he is "Tom," a unique individual, wholly himself. This aspect of Tom exists in time, as Eldest.

On the other hand, he is nameless, he simply is. He is consciousness before it splits and creates individual ego identity; he is unconditioned, timeless Self, utterly immersed in Eternal Now, at one with the unending dark under the stars.

CHAPTER 12

Tom Has No Fear

Tom "knew the dark under the stars when it was fearless — before the Dark Lord came from outside." The arrival of the Dark Lord "from outside" symbolizes the primordial creation of a separate self. In contrast to the seamless, undivided, timeless Self, the Dark Lord enters from "outside" the Oneness of the world. He is split off from Oneness, representing an ego consciousness that knows only its separateness and has forgotten its original and still extant Oneness.

Early in the development of our personal psyche — after our merged, pre-personal experience of oneness in our mother's womb — it is important and necessary that slowly we begin to differentiate as a separate ego personality. When we are in our prepersonal merged state, without an other, without something that is "not-me," there is nothing to fear. However, as noted above, once there is a separate self to protect, then fear naturally arises. So long as we continue to identify solely as a separate self, fear persists. The path of maturation eventually points us beyond this level of narcissistic identification and toward remembering our original undivided Self – only in adulthood it is a *transpersonal* experience of Oneness that both transcends and includes an awareness of our individuality. This experience of Oneness exists in marked contrast to the early, undifferentiated, pre-personal merging characteristic of the newborn. The transpersonal experience of Oneness is a stage of maturation we may experience intermittently, or – less commonly – as a relatively stable and abiding awareness.

Bombadil is a marvelous exemplar of the transpersonal undivided Self. Goldberry says of her husband, "He has no fear," and she tells the Hobbits also to "Fear nothing! For tonight you are under the roof of Tom Bombadil." (Tolkien, 1965a, page 134) In Middle-Earth, Bombadil alone is not afraid to make mention of the Dark Lord, even going so far, as we shall see, to make light of him and of the Ring of Power.

Bombadil's lack of fear, and Goldberry's exhortation to the Hobbits to "Fear nothing!" recalls an essential teaching of Christianity, Buddhism and Hinduism, all of which, in their wisdom lineage, teach about the transpersonal experience of oneness. Many times, in both the Old and New Testaments the words "Fear not" are repeated. In Buddhism, Prajnaparamita, the Mother of the Buddhas who represents unconditioned consciousness, "keeps saying, 'Don't be afraid.' In painted and sculpted forms, she holds her hand, palm outward, in the gesture that means, 'Fear not.'" (Macy, 1995, page 6) A passage from the Brihadaranyaka Upanishad succinctly comments on the root cause of fear, "It is from a second entity that fear comes." (*Brihadaranyaka Upanishad,* page I-iv-2)

Tom Bombadil – living as nonseparate, undivided Self – knows no Other; hence he has no fear.

CHAPTER 13

The Invisibility of
The Ring-Bearer

In *The Lord of the Rings,* whoever wears the Ring becomes invisible to – and therefore symbolically separate from – others. We already have seen how the Ring represents Sauron's narcissistic injury (or core wound) and his consequent rage. Exploring the Ring's power to evoke this "separating" invisibility will enable us more fully to understand the power that the narcissistic injury holds over the ego personality. In addition, it will – by contrast – further illuminate Tom Bombadil's transparency of character, for Tom has no need, or desire, to be hidden.

Sauron's Ring / narcissistic injury essentially is invisible to him despite the powerful hold it has on every aspect of his life. His "Eye" roves Middle Earth, searching for his Ring / injury. He is looking the wrong direction. Sauron's wound festers deep within, yet he is aware of it only insofar as his rage and desire for vengeance are a felt reaction to it. This is a far cry, however, from truly having the capacity to *see and feel into the heart of his wound.* Sauron's unrelenting violence and fury are clear signs that he has not felt and faced his core wound fully, directly, and consciously, thereby witnessing and releasing the depth of his pain. Instead, we see him avoiding and defending against his pain by becoming consumed with blinding anger against others. Metaphorically, then, Sauron's Ring represents his narcissistic injury, and its "cloaking" capability represents the tendency of the core wound injury to remain unconscious — *and thus invisible* — to the ego personality.

Sauron's "unseeing" denial of his own narcissistic injury is not unusual. Whenever any of us experiences the profound vulnerability of core wound pain — a pain so penetrating it feels as though it threatens our very existence — the urge to avert our gaze becomes almost irresistibly compelling. Our instinctive avoidance serves as our own "cloak of invisibility" for masking our narcissistic injury. Like Sauron, we are run by that which we refuse to see and feel, and which we then project into the world. There are very few that have allowed themselves to be uncloaked by transparency and truth; few that have had the courage to face — and see into — the depth of core wound pain, and to have found beneath it the peace that always is present. It is a peace fundamentally unshaken by the terrible wounding we encounter in the world.

In the magical tapestry of Tolkien's novels, proximity with the Ring has several effects on any Ring-bearer and on those around him:

First, we find that Sauron's narcissistic injury — now projected into the Ring — will amplify the felt-pain of any Ring-bearer's own narcissistic injury. As a consequence, like Sauron, the Ring-bearer's temptation to avoid the pain of his narcissistic injury is heightened. Further intensified is the

Ring-bearer's temptation to succumb to the seduction of power as an apparent means of avoiding this pain. *Thus, the Ring is both the cause of the Ring-bearer's greater suffering and is an addictive and illusory means of dealing with that suffering.*

Next, as also was true for Sauron, although magnifying the felt-pain of the narcissistic injury, the Ring, paradoxically, amplifies the *invisibility* – i.e., unconsciousness – of the Ring-bearer's core wound. Thus, the Ring-as-narcissistic-injury has a cloaking effect, and this cloaking power affects *both Ring-bearer and observer alike.* The Ring-bearer already is beset by an unavoidable sense of separateness from the world that is characteristic of any ego personality. Donning the Ring amplifies that painfully heavy sense of separation, symbolically represented as invisibility. But the effects of the Ring do not stop there. Putting on the Ring not only magnifies the Ring-bearer's own "blindness" to and separation from himself *but also amplifies it into an interpersonal process* by rendering him separate from and invisible to others. This is because the core wound's "cloak of invisibility" – i.e., its tendency to remain unconscious – is echoed within other ego personalities. Anyone whose narcissistic injury remains invisible (i.e., unconscious) to themselves also will find the Ring-bearer to be invisible.

Paradoxically, then, to wear the Ring is to stand before everyone as overt symbol of the core wound, and yet, ironically, to be invisible. The Ring-bearer simultaneously is one who cannot clearly see himself (because his core wound is activated by the Ring) *and* one who cannot clearly be seen by others (because their core wounds likewise are activated). The result is a profound, yet commonly felt, sense of human alienation.

The invisibility of the Ring-bearer is a powerful metaphor for ordinary human life. We stand before each other, deeply affected by our core wounds, wearing invisible "Rings" (i.e., unconscious, split-off aspects of our personality) that both *signify* and *cloak* the depth of our wounding, such that we remain largely invisible to ourselves and to each other. Controlled and blinded by our unconscious wounds, we cannot see each other as we truly are; instead, we become wraith-selves within – and also with one another. Our invisibility may suggest possessing a certain kind of "power," but it is in itself injurious, for in order to be healed, the narcissistic injury needs compassionately to be seen and held in vulnerability and transparency, not only by ourselves, but, in all likelihood, by others as well.

On one level, the effects of our core wounds visibly are manifest throughout the world, often, echoing Sauron, appearing in myriad forms of overt human violence. It is more difficult, however, to connect our narcissistic injuries with less obvious signs that can appear as dysfunctional family interactions, chronic health issues, substance abuse, overeating, chronic depression and suicide, to name but a few. Typically, our internal pain and sense of separateness is too great to bear, and so early on we learn to cover it over, thus making it invisible to ourselves and to others. Our personal "Ring," hiding under the shine of our polished personas, allows us to stay hidden to ourselves even while, like Sauron, blindly seeking to impose our own particular version of egoic perfection, order and control on the world.

CHAPTER 14

Why Tom is Impervious to The Ring

Bombadil has utterly no interest in the power embodied in the Ring. His transparency of being is his true power, and he has no need for hiddenness or invisibility. The first thing he does when Frodo hands him the Ring is suddenly to put it up to his eye, look through its opening, and laugh. With this surprising gesture he makes light of the red Eye of Sauron, the dread symbol of Sauron's evil attention and intent. Instead of being transfixed by the Ring (as is the case for all others who view it), he literally and figuratively "sees right through" and beyond the corrupting lust for power that constellates around the Ring. (Treschow and Duckworth, 2006, page 185) As Goldberry pointed out, Tom cannot be "caught."

In contrast to all other characters in The Lord of the Rings, Tom alone is impervious to the power of the Ring, and he demonstrates this to great effect when he puts it on his finger yet remains visible. This elicits a gasp from the Hobbits. Later, when Frodo puts on the Ring, he remains completely visible to Tom, and only to Tom. This is because Tom is not split off from the world – he is one with it. We have seen that the Ring amplifies the tendency of the ego personality to feel separate and split off from the world, but this has no effect on Tom's unconditioned Self. He is one with himself and one with the world, and the Ring cannot sever that inherent and essential connection.

Tom plays with the Ring as though it were a bauble – which, to him, it is – by making the Ring itself disappear and reappear. To him, the Ring represents a game people play with themselves, feeling as though they are separate from the world while desperately trying to achieve some control over it. This game has no sway over Bombadil and it holds no interest for him. He is beyond the stage at which power is a compelling force, operating as he does from the perspective of the unconditioned Self rather than the ego personality. As such, he can view and even wear the Ring – the symbol of power, control, obsession and ego aggrandizement – while standing completely outside of its sphere of influence. Tom reflects to us a basic psychospiritual truth: as we progress in psychospiritual maturity, events that previously would have affected us profoundly no longer have the power to distract or capture our attention. We can learn how to "spin them in the air" and make them "vanish with a flash" – as does Tom with the Ring.

CHAPTER 15

Tom's Inherent Joy of Being

Because he is surrendered to and not in any way separate from life, Tom embodies and expresses spontaneous joy. Tolkien describes Bombadil as one who "take[s] delight in things for themselves." (Carpenter, 1981, page 179) While in his company, the Hobbits discover that Tom's joy is contagious: "The drink in their drinking-bowls seemed to be clear cold water, yet it went to their hearts like wine and set free their voices. The guests became suddenly aware that they were singing merrily, as if it was easier and more natural than talking." (Tolkien, 1965a, page 136)

Tom's happiness is not childish; rather, it is the pure, inherent joy of Being. As Eckhart Tolle remarks, "The joy of Being, which is the only true happiness, cannot come to you through any form, possession, achievement, person, or event — through anything that happens. That joy cannot come to you — ever. It emanates from the formless dimension within you, from consciousness itself and thus is one with who you are." (Tolle, 2005, page 214)

Because Tom is spontaneous, exuberant and displays a

"childlike" happiness, some authors have portrayed him as a naïve innocent, casting him as a kind of Adam figure (at least as Adam mostly has been understood and portrayed), and depicting the realm he lives in as a Middle-Earth version of Eden. But Tom's realm is not a simple and innocent paradise, and Tom profoundly understands the truth of life's mysteries, shadows and brokenness. There are dangers, both close to his home as well as beyond the borders of his realm. He is cognizant of the battle for the Ring, but chooses, for the most part, to stand outside the struggle. (It is important to note, however, that the actions he does take – saving the Hobbits on several occasions, and providing them with magical swords – prove to be crucial to the success of their quest. These and other actions of his demonstrate that he is supportive of those who do not wish dominion over others.) So, although Tom often has a carefree manner, he is far from being unconscious and naïve. While the Hobbits were his guests,

> He then told them many remarkable stories, sometimes half as if speaking to himself, sometimes looking at them suddenly with a bright blue eye under his deep brows. Often his voice would turn to song, and he would get out of his chair and dance about. He told them tales of bees and flowers, the ways of trees, and the strange creatures of the Forest, about evil things and good things, things friendly and things unfriendly, cruel things and kind things, and secrets hidden under brambles.
>
> (Tolkien, 1965a, pages 140–141)

Unlike Adam, who in the womb of Eden was not yet privy to the ways of the world, Tom knows of the Dark Lord from the outside, of evil, cruelty, and unfriendly things, and he acts as a teacher for the Hobbits. Unlike Adam, Tom knows the history of the world intimately. He has lived and witnessed it, even while dwelling in the Eternal Now. Where Adam can be seen to represent pre-personal inexperience, Tom represents a mature, trans-personal blend of joy, wonder and wisdom.

Tom's wisdom of the world is born of intimate communion – he is one with all he knows. Resting in Being, he inhabits the world at the level of existence itself, prior to thought and individual preference. The range, depth and intimacy of Tom's knowledge and wisdom is far beyond the Hobbits, and they can feel this; therefore, they can feel, by contrast, how they are "strangers," living "outside" of a fully intimate, nonseparate relationship with the world.

> "As they [the Hobbits] listened, they began to understand the lives of the Forest, apart from themselves, indeed feel themselves as the strangers where all other things were at home."
>
> (Tolkien, 1965a, page 140)

Of course the Hobbits do experience a degree of intimacy with the world, through their love of the Shire, of food, of each other, and so forth, but their intimacy is at a much different level of development than Tom's. The Hobbits can be seen, then, as representing the inherent separation of any ego personality, while Tom represents the inherent connectedness of the unconditioned Self.

CHAPTER 16

Tom Bombadil is Master

When Frodo originally asks Goldberry about Tom, her answer – "He is" – is not sufficient for him. She adds,

"He is, as you have seen him . . . He is the Master of wood, water, and hill."

"Then all this strange land belongs to him?"

"No indeed!" She answered, and her smile faded. "That would indeed be a burden," she added in a low voice, as if to herself. "The trees and the grasses and all things growing or living in the land belong each to themselves. Tom Bombadil is the Master. No one has ever caught old Tom walking in the forest, wading in the water, leaping on the hilltops under light and shadow. He has no fear. Tom Bombadil is master."

(Tolkien, 1965a, page 135)

Tom is "Master," in a very special sense of the word, and this too sets him apart from all of the other characters in

The Lord of the Rings. In Tom Bombadil, Tolkien created a character that is an example of liberation from personality. There is no question that Tom has a distinctive – and quirky – persona, but the essence of his identity is more than or beyond his personality. He is *trans*-personal, dwelling in the deeper truth of who he is. The unconditioned Self lives in, as and through him.

Tom's identity always is paradoxical. On the one hand, he is "Master" of himself because he is not identified with, and therefore bound by, his ego personality. He is free from his personality as well as free to spontaneously express himself through his personality. On the other hand, Tom cannot be "Master" of himself because, as the unconditioned Self, he does not have a "self" of which he can be master. We only can "master" something that is separate from ourselves, and Tom is not separate from anything, including himself. So, Tom is Master and yet nothing "belongs" to him. His "mastery," therefore, comes from a complete surrender of the separate self of ego personality. At Tom's level of development – i.e., resting in Being – mastery has a very different connotation than it does from the vantage point of the ego personality, for Tom has no *need* for power and mastery over anything or anyone. As Goldberry remarks, "That would indeed be a burden." This is, in fact, the onerous burden of the Ring, whereas Tom is that rare and true Master who is free to be a servant to all of life.

In all of his qualities – his inherent connectedness and goodwill, his joy, his complete immersion in the present, his lack of fear, his complete disinterest in power, and his humble respect for life – Tom is Being itself. We could say that he is the antithesis of Sauron, and in many respects that is true. It also is true that Tom's nonseparate nature, wisdom and ubiquitous Being place him in a completely different paradigm altogether. For Sauron, Tom is beyond comprehension; but for Tom, even one such as Sauron is not separate from the all-encompassing embrace of "I Am."

CHAPTER 17

Tolkien's Understanding Of Bombadil's True Nature

There is no way to know with certainty the degree to which Tolkien understood the nature of the character he created in Tom Bombadil. Although it is beyond the scope of this book to explore this topic in great detail, we would like to offer a few brief speculations.

The clearest indication that Tolkien understood Bombadil's deeper nature is to be found in his reflections about the central theme of *The Lord of the Rings*. In Letter 144, written in April 1954, some six years after he had completed *The Lord of the Rings*, Tolkien conceives of his novel as a battle for power and control between "a good side, and a bad side." (Carpenter, 1981, page 178) In a letter written a year later, his perspective begins to undergo a significant shift. Once again Tolkien addresses the primary themes of his book, but this time he reveals a deeper level of discernment, one that is directly relevant to the character of Bombadil, the nature of the One Ring and the challenge it poses.

Tolkien begins Letter 186 in April 1956 by echoing Letter 144, writing that ". . . my story is . . . an allegory . . . of *Power* (exerted for Domination). . . ." (Carpenter, 1981, page 246) Then, reflecting further, he quickly amends this point of view:

> "I do not think that even Power or Domination is the real centre of my story. It provides the theme of a War, about something dark and threatening enough to seem at that time of supreme importance, but that is mainly 'a setting' for characters to show themselves. The real theme for me is about something much more permanent and difficult: Death and Immortality . . ."
>
> (Carpenter, 1981, page 246)

This marks a major shift in Tolkien's understanding of *The Lord of the Rings.* He now is focused on the idea that whereas wars (with their emphasis on power and domination) are transitory, the question of man's relationship with death and immortality is ever-present.

Two years later, in April 1958, he returns to the topic of immortality, making a crucial observation: "I said, or meant to say, that the 'message' was the hideous peril of confusing true 'immortality' with limitless serial longevity. Freedom from Time, and clinging to Time." (Carpenter, 1981, page 267) Tolkien echoes and elaborates upon these remarks six months later:

> But I might say that if the tale is 'about' anything (other than itself), it is not as seems widely supposed about 'power'. Power-seeking is only the motive –

power that sets events going, and is relatively unimportant, I think. It is mainly concerned with Death,
and Immortality; and the 'escapes': serial longevity,
and hoarding memory.

(Carpenter, 1981, page 267)

There is a significant change of view from that originally
expressed in Letter 144, written in 1954, in which the
struggle for power and control was seen as the central
theme. By 1956 Tolkien believes that the desire for power
and domination is "mainly 'a setting' for characters to
show themselves" and is "only the motive-power that sets
events going, and is relatively unimportant . . ." Then, in
1958, he identifies the deeper issue, which he views as the
more fundamental test for his characters, as "the hideous
peril of confusing true 'immortality' with limitless serial
longevity." "True immortality," as Tolkien understands it, is
"freedom from Time," in contrast to limitless serial longevity, which is "clinging to Time."

These passages seem to demonstrate Tolkien's own evo-
lution of thought over a period of four years. Tolkien indi-
cates an arrival at a deepening understanding that the
desire for power and domination are a vehicle to a false
sense of immortality. The addictive quest for ever-
increasing power and domination are an expression of the
personality's desire to control life, and thereby *defy death.*
The irony of course is that this desperate grasping – vainly
striving to maintain a kind of stasis in an impermanent
world – this "clinging to Time," is itself a kind of death,
and thus the "hideous peril" alluded to by Tolkien. By contrast, when the small "me" of the ego personality has been
transcended, then the unconditioned Self – utterly surren-

dered to the unfolding Eternal Now – experiences "true immortality" and "freedom from Time."

This distinction is directly relevant to the character of Tom Bombadil. Bombadil alone, amongst the figures in *The Lord of the Rings*, lives in the Eternal Now and thus, in that sense, is immortal. All the other characters, to one degree or another, feeling themselves to be separate, vulnerable, and mortal, struggle with their desire to possess the corrupting power of the Ring in order to have personal control of their earthly fate. Some succumb to the lure of the Ring, thereby clinging to time and a spiritually empty longevity, while others resist, allowing for a deepening toward the immutable, eternal Beingness exemplified by Bombadil.

Tolkien demonstrated his understanding of our human relationship to immortality in several ways: First, through his dramatic enactment of the lure of the One Ring and the temptation it exerted on the characters of the Lord of the Rings. Second, by creating Tom Bombadil as an exemplar of one who is spiritually surrendered to and living in the Eternal Now, and who has no interest, therefore, in the powers the Ring can bestow. Third, through observations he made in his personal letters after *The Lord of the Rings* had been published.

Tolkien's letters are a strong indication that his conscious understanding of this particular theme developed after the books were complete. This is in accord with his disclosure in Letter 211 that, in general, his conscious understanding of and intention to create the many layers of meaning in *The Lord of the Rings* was minimal during the actual writing:

> "*The Lord of the Rings* as a story was finished so long ago now that I can take a largely impersonal

view of it, and find 'interpretations' quite amusing;
even those that I might make myself, which are
mostly post scriptum: I had very little particular,
conscious, intellectual, intention in mind at any
point."

(Carpenter, 1981, page 211)

Tolkien does not relate his understanding of immortality
specifically to Bombadil, but it is this insight that is most
relevant to Bombadil's deeper nature. It is a core recognition that is explained lucidly in the second chapter of the
Bhagavad Gita:

*When you keep thinking about sense-objects
attachment comes. Attachment breeds desire, the
lust of possession that burns to anger. Anger
clouds the judgment; you can no longer learn
from past mistakes. Lost is the power to choose
between what is wise and what is unwise, and your
life is utter waste. But when you move amidst
the world of sense, free from attachment and aversion
alike, there comes the peace in which all sorrows
end, and you live in the wisdom of the Self . . .*

*They are forever free who renounce all
selfish desires and break away from the ego-cage
of "I," "me," and "mine" . . .
This is the supreme state. Attain to
this, and pass from death to immortality.*

(Bhagavad Gita 96-97)

Tolkien was inspired to give to the world a vast, vivid and compelling portrayal of the addictive grasping for power and its false sense of immortality – a grasping to which, to varying degrees, we all fall prey. Although it appears that he was not fully conscious of doing so while writing *The Lord of the Rings*, Tolkien subtly has juxtaposed that kind of power-hungry avarice with Tom Bombadil's "I Am" – a timeless, joyful, resting in and as Being itself that is the essential truth of Who we all are.

CHAPTER 18

Who is Tom Bombadil?

"Remember, mystery isn't something that you cannot understand – it is something that you can endlessly understand! There is no point at which you can say, 'I've got it.' Always and forever, mystery gets you!"
–Richard Rohr, *The Divine Dance*

Who, really, is Tom Bombadil?

Tom is mystery – *as are we all*. We can project many things upon him – but the essential and extraordinary invitation is to see that we *are* him.

We, like Tom, can openly choose to enter the mystery of our being with deepening understanding. Gazing into Tom's iconic face, we see, mirrored back, who we truly are.

We are freedom.

We are love.

We are Being itself.

Like Tom, as the true and unconditioned Self, we are free to see through the prevailing power structures and strictures in our world, and the ways that world attempts to seduce and define us. We can "see through" such Rings, discerning the truth of our unconscious bondage to addictive systems and perverted power. Then, we can turn and walk deeper into Nature – our own true Nature, as well as the visible natural world that holds and nourishes us all. In so doing, we return to the home that we have never left, and never can leave: our oneness with everything.

With courage and clear intention, we begin to see as Tom sees, uncovering the places where we cloak ourselves, acting invisible, whether through constraints inherent in our ego-identities, or through this world's dominating systems. These are the hiding places where we feel isolated, inadequate, filled with fear, heavy with oppression, tortured, trapped and doomed by the seeming stranglehold of all that seeks to bind us.

Let us reach for and discover the true Self and inherent freedom that forever is untouched by outdated architectures of false potency – rather than succumbing to their gripping, chilling effect on our lives. Let us, with Tom, metaphorically and *literally* laugh, dance and sing once again in the face of such "power" and "powers."

How can we live simply and beautifully, plant gardens, restore and care for the Earth and all of her species – tenderly nurture one another?

This is not about being naïve – as Tom is neither naïve nor unaware of the darkness gathering in the world. He does not turn away from such knowledge. As Tolkien's characters demonstrate, it takes courage and true fellowship – brave and authentic community – to keep moving with fortitude through increasing levels of malevolence and power gone awry. Tom supports this journey *and* teaches us the paradox we need to hold it all. Through clear seeing, through his very *being* – he shares with us a profoundly rooted Story, a joyful engagement with life and the potent freedom of truth. Tom lovingly plants and tends to life in the midst of his great knowledge of looming darkness. He shows us it is possible to see and not shrink from – to fully acknowledge yet not be blinded and controlled by – the darkness.

We have a journey to take – a dynamic adventure to unfold. We begin by telling one another the fathomless truth of WHO we are . . . begin to live this truth as love, evoking empowering stories about our fellowship – our marriage of oneness – with stars and trees and skies, the deep earth . . . and all that is.

Step by step, in solitary contemplation and beloved community, we awaken, *re-*member – reassemble – all of the torn asunder fragments of our own bodies and psyches, of humanity's body, of the world's body.

We begin, as Tom, with the mystery of simplicity. Begin with I Am.

Works Cited

Almaas, A.H. (1996). *The Point of Existence.* Berkeley: Diamond Books.

Bhagavad Gita, Eknath Easwaran, trans. (2007). Tomales, CA: Nilgiri Press. 2nd edition, 68-69

Brihadaranyaka Upanishad, Swami Madhavananda trans. (1965). Calcutta: Advaita Ashrama.

Buechner, Frederick (1973). *Wishful Thinking: A Theological ABC.* New York: Harper & Row.

Carpenter, Humphrey, ed. (1981). *The Letters of J. R. R. Tolkien*, Boston: Houghton Mifflin.

Engler, John H. (1993). "Becoming Somebody and Nobody: Psychoanalysis and Buddhism." *Paths Beyond Ego: The Transpersonal Vision.* Walsh, Roger and Vaughan, Frances, eds. New York: Tarcher/Putnam.

Epstein, Mark (1995). *Thoughts Without a Thinker: Psychotherapy from a Buddhist Perspective.* New York: Basic Books.

Fisher, Mark(n.d.). *The Riddle of Tom Bombadil.* The Encyclopedia of Arda, retrieved from http://www.glyphweb.com/arda/t/tombombadil.html.

Kohut, Heinz (1978). "Thoughts on Narcissism and Narcissistic Rage." *The Search for the Self, Volume 2.* New York: International Universities Press, Inc.

Macy, Joanna (1995). "The Incredible Exploding Self: An Interview with Joanna Macy," *Inquiring Mind* 11/2, Spring.

Nisargadatta (2005). *I Am That.* Frydman, Maurice, trans. Durham, N. Carolina: The Acorn Press.

Tolkien, J. R. R., and Christopher Tolkien (1993). *Morgoth's Ring: The Later Silmarillion, Part 1, the Legends of Aman.* Boston: Houghton Mifflin.

———, J.R.R. (1965a). *The Fellowship of the Ring.* Boston: Houghton Mifflin.

———, J.R.R. (1965b). *The Return of the King.* Boston: Houghton Mifflin.

———, J.R.R. (2002). *The Silmarillion, 2nd ed.* New York, Ballantine Books.

Tolle, Eckhart (2005). *A New Earth.* New York: Plume.

———, Eckhart (2006). Stillness Speaks. New York: Christian Large Print.

Treschow, Michael, and Duckworth, Mark (2006). "Bombadil's Role in *The Lord of the Rings.*" Mythlore 25:1/2 Fall/Winter.

Upanishads, Part 2 (SBE15) (2006). Müller, Friedrich Max trans. Boston: Adamant Media Corporation.

Walsh, Fran; Jackson, Peter; Boyens, Philippa (2001). *The Lord of the Rings: The Fellowship of the Rings.* Movie script, retrieved from http://www.imsdb.com/scripts/Lord-of-the-Rings-Fellowship-of-the-Ring%2C-The.html

About the Authors

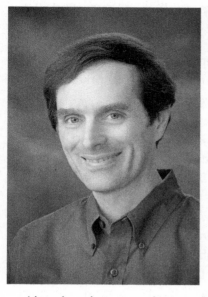

ALAN JAMES STRACHAN, Ph.D., is a psychotherapist, teacher and author. (www.alanstrachan.com)

Alan graduated *summa cum laude* with an interdisciplinary undergraduate degree, and then earned two Master's degrees and a Ph.D. in psychology. He has been in private practice as a psychotherapist for over 30 years, and was the staff counselor at the Stanford Research Institute (SRI International) for 9 years.

Alan has been exploring the interface between psychology and spirituality for over 40 years. He has taught for 30 years at university and corporate settings, as well as at professional gatherings such as the Association for Transpersonal Psychology and the Nondual Wisdom and Psychology conferences. He has maintained a meditation practice for 35 years, and for many years Alan and his wife Janet facilitated a support group for people on the spiritual path.

Alan weaves his personal integration of nonduality with an ongoing interest in psychotherapy as spiritual practice, and he is co-author of the forthcoming book, provisionally entitled *The Psychology of Liberation and the Liberation of Psychology: Psychotherapy as Spiritual Practice.* He is also keenly interested in exploring the intersection between psychology, spirituality and politics (www.americaonthecouch.net).

When not obsessing about the meaning of life, Alan delights in walking in nature, sharing meals with friends, shaking with laughter, and yelling at the television during the NBA finals.

JANET COSTER, M.A., M.A., is a transpersonal counselor, spiritual director and workshop leader. She is certified in Spiritual Direction, Authentic Movement and Gender Reconciliation and has been in private practice for over 20 years.

In 2006 Janet was part of a staff facilitation team offering an Intensive 5-Day Workshop in Gender Reconciliation in Capetown South Africa, which included Members of Parliament, Members of the South African Council of Churches and Members of NGO Women's Circles. She has co-facilitated workshops in the US since then.

In addition to her counseling practice, Janet is a poet, songwriter and singer, and has a semi-professional background with many years spent, both as director and performer in dance and theater. She was a cofounder of Hit and Run Theater in Santa Cruz, CA.

Janet's counseling, teaching and writing are deeply influenced by a lifelong spiritual practice. A significant deepening occurred around 25 years ago when she experienced a prolonged period of spiritual awakening, a process of being completely shattered – and also of completely falling in love with everything and everyone – all at the same time. She has since experienced an extended integration of that awakening, a Dark Night transit in which everything that does not appear as Love has arisen to be seen, and seen through, from the awakened perspective.

For eight years Janet co-facilitated a weekly support group for people on the spiritual path with her husband Alan. They have published a number of articles online, and soon will be publishing several books focusing on the intersection of psychology, spirituality and politics.

Janet balances the more focused aspects of her spiritual practice with a delight in dance, wordplay and chocolate, irreverent humor, impromptu impersonations, and periodic threats to write a blog deconstructing the melodrama of the NBA.

Made in the USA
Las Vegas, NV
23 May 2021

23554252R00052